TO ALL THE CHILDREN OF THE WORLD, BIG AND SMALL
—R.F. & T.B.

FOR DARCY AND OLLIE
—H.G.

Text copyright © 2023 by Roberta Flack and Tonya Bolden
Jacket art and interior illustrations copyright © 2023 by Hayden Goodman

All rights reserved. Published in the United States by Anne Schwartz Books, an imprint of Random House Children's
Books, a division of Penguin Random House LLC, New York.
Anne Schwartz Books and the colophon are trademarks of Penguin Random House LLC.

Visit us on the Web! rhcbooks.com
Educators and librarians, for a variety of teaching tools, visit us at RHTeachersLibrarians.com

Library of Congress Cataloging-in-Publication Data is available upon request.
ISBN 978-0-593-47987-2 (trade) — ISBN 978-0-593-47988-9 (lib. bdg.) — ISBN 978-0-593-47989-6 (ebook)

The text of this book is set in 13-point Chronicle Text.
The illustrations are gouache paintings, with some finishing details rendered digitally.
Book design by Sarah Hokanson

MANUFACTURED IN CHINA
10 9 8 7 6 5 4 3 2 1 First Edition

The Green Piano

How Little Me Found Music

ROBERTA FLACK WITH **TONYA BOLDEN**

ILLUSTRATED BY **HAYDEN GOODMAN**

a·s·b

anne schwartz books

Little me, in my Blue Ridge Mountain town
of Asheville, North Carolina,
living on a street named Velvet,
then on one named Circle,
I didn't have fancy-fine clothes,

high-priced toys,
or other richy-rich
things.

But I had music.

My treasure.
My gold.

Daddy—
his name was Laron—
at one time a waiter,
at one time a cook,
and later a builder,
had taught himself to play piano.
Harmonica, too.

Mother—
her name was Irene—
a maid for a time,
had taken some music lessons as a child
and now played the organ so nicely at our church.
Piano, too.

At age three, maybe four,
there was me
at the keys
of that church piano.

I'd use my elbows on the ebonies
because my fingers were too short.
Mother and Daddy were so tickled by that—
and so proud of me.

I imagined an entire congregation listening to me play
hymns like "Precious Lord, Take My Hand,"
and even songs I heard on the radio,
like "A-Tisket, A-Tasket."

And I dreamed of having my very own piano.

Dreamed of my own piano when I tap-tap-tapped
out tunes

on tabletops,

windowsills.

Dreamed of that piano when,
with my slight voice,
I sailed into sing-alongs
with big sister Nancy,
with little sister LaRene.

"Twinkle, Twinkle, Little Star" was a favorite.

Older me, age six,
started taking piano lessons,
from a mighty fine lady with a noble-sounding name,
Mrs. Hightower.

And when Mrs. Hightower
heard that we were moving—

"You must make sure Roberta
continues her piano lessons when you get up there!"

Up there was Virginia,
in a place called Green Valley,
in a home where
Mother, Daddy, neighbors, friends made music
     together,
offering up soul-soothing harmonica tunes,
playing the spoons,
singing love right into our living room.
With me still, *still* dreaming of my very own piano.

Then one day, not many miles away, in Washington, DC,
Daddy spied something in a junkyard he was passing by.
Something that brought a glistening to his eyes.
Something he just *knew* would make nine-year-old me
burst into a thousand smiles.

A piano.

A small upright piano.

Old, ratty, beat-up, weather-worn, faded thing.
Its ivories terribly stained.
And it stank!
But Daddy, he saw treasure,
saw gold.

"Can I have it?" he eagerly asked Mr. Junkyard Man.

"Come and get it," the man replied with a shrug.

Lickety-split, Daddy hustled up help to haul that piano home.

When I first saw my piano,
I saw a miracle.

Daddy put his *all* into fixing up that old,
ratty, beat-up,
weather-worn,
faded,
stained,
stinky thing.

When can I play it?!

That was me as he cleaned it,
cleaned it,
cleaned it,
with Mother lending
a helping hand.

When can I play it?!

That was me as he tuned it.

When can I play it?!

That was me as Daddy painted that
  piano a grassy green.

I couldn't wait, couldn't *wait,* couldn't WAIT for
  the paint to dry!

And then . . .

Gently, I touched the keys,
my green piano
already a part of me,
notes flowing through my fingers
to my body,
to my soul.

I practiced for hours and hours.
Teaching myself to play songs
from the radio,
like "Let It Snow! Let It Snow! Let It Snow!"
Teaching myself to play songs
from church,
like "Amazing Grace."
Taking piano lessons again, from Alma Blackmon,
a top teacher in DC.

Soon my fingers,
longer, stronger,
graceful,
were gliding into songs,
like Beethoven's Moonlight Sonata,
like Handel's *Messiah*.

Soon when I sang along to songs,
my voice was
no longer slight, but
      stronger
      richer,
      smoother.

And soon I had an even bigger dream.

Of a life
all wrapped up in
the majesty,
the magic
of music—
my treasure,
my gold.

Grown-up me lived this dream!
Year after year after year!

Along the way, I never forgot
the joy,
the miracle,
the wonder,
the blessing
of
my
green piano.

AUTHOR'S NOTE

When I was growing up in Green Valley in the 1940s, I never dreamed of becoming a singer.

As I played my green piano, studied with the amazing Alma Blackmon, and accompanied the choir at my family's church, I dreamed of performing on grand stages, playing the works of Beethoven and other composers of classical music. I dreamed of becoming a concert pianist.

That was my dream at Hoffman-Boston High School, where my senior class voted me the "most musical." That was my dream when I entered Howard University at the age of fifteen on a full music scholarship. That was *still* my dream when I graduated in 1958 with a bachelor's degree in music education.

But life had other plans for me.

Four years later, in 1962, I was teaching music at a junior high school in Washington, DC. Thanks to Miss Alma, I also landed a part-time job playing the piano at the Tivoli Opera Restaurant in Georgetown.

I loved being around those opera singers, so much so that I began taking voice lessons with the legendary Frederick "Wilkie" Wilkerson. But one day Wilkie told me, "Your voice is better for pop music than for opera."

I was crushed!

I walked away from Wilkie, walked away from song. Then, after some reflection, I thought, *Maybe he's right!* Back to Wilkie I went, and I learned to sing popular songs of the time. I found my voice.

One night at Tivoli, after all the guests had gone, Henry Yaffe, the owner, overheard me singing a mellow song to the opera singers. "You can sing that stuff at intermissions," he said. And so I did.

Before long, I was singing on Sunday afternoons in Henry's ground-floor club, Mr. Henry's, on Capitol Hill. I saw that people were moved by my singing, and I wanted to do more. After Henry agreed to let me perform three nights a week, I resigned from teaching to devote all my energy to music, music, music!

Devote myself to practicing, practicing, practicing!

Devote myself to giving every performance my all, connecting with the audience through songs about sorrows, joy, and love!

From the blues and rock to folk, soul, and jazz—I sang it all.

My audience grew so large that Henry created "Roberta's Room" upstairs in his club. There, I sang and played the piano, backed by a bass player, a drummer, and eventually a guitarist—five nights a week, three shows a night. It was exhausting but exhilarating at the same time!

The great jazz pianist and singer Les McCann came to see me in a benefit concert I gave for a local childcare center and worked overtime to get me an audition with Atlantic Records. That led to my first album, *First Take,* released in 1969, which included "The First Time Ever I Saw Your Face." The song became a hit!

Over the years, I was blessed to sing more songs that became hits and won awards. I performed all over the country—and all over the world.

I also gave back. In 2006, I established the Roberta Flack School of Music at the Hyde Leadership Charter School in the Bronx, in New York City, offering free music education to elementary and middle schoolers. A few years later came the Roberta Flack Foundation, devoted to, among other things, helping children—especially girls of color—with their music education. Through this amazing journey of mine, that once-little me who so cherished her green piano was always by my side.

I decided to tell the story about my green piano because I want all the young people who have ever felt marginalized, overwhelmed, bullied, or discriminated against to know that they can make their dreams come true. Find your own "green piano" and practice relentlessly until you find your voice, and a way to put that beautiful music into the world.

Roberta at 7 years old   Roberta at 14 years old

CAREER HIGHLIGHTS

1967: Roberta begins singing professionally at Henry Yaffe's club on Capitol Hill.

1968: Roberta receives her first recording contract.

1969: Roberta's first album, *First Take,* is released.

1971: Roberta performs at Carnegie Hall. • *Play Misty for Me,* Clint Eastwood's film about a DJ, is released. The soundtrack includes "The First Time Ever I Saw Your Face."

1973: "The First Time Ever I Saw Your Face" wins a Grammy for Record of the Year. • "Where Is the Love," a duet with Howard University classmate Donny Hathaway, wins the Grammy for Best Pop Vocal Performance by a Duo, Group, or Chorus.

1974: "Killing Me Softly with His Song" wins Grammys for Record of the Year and Best Pop Vocal Performance—Female. • Roberta wins an American Music Award for Favorite Female Artist—Soul/R&B.

1979: Roberta wins another American Music Award for Favorite Female Artist—Soul/R&B.

1999: Roberta is honored with a star on the Hollywood Walk of Fame. • "Killing Me Softly with His Song" is inducted into the Grammy Hall of Fame.

2009: Roberta is inducted into the North Carolina Music Hall of Fame.

2016: Roberta's first album, *First Take,* is inducted into Grammy Hall of Fame.

2020: Roberta receives the Grammy Lifetime Achievement Award.

2021: Roberta is inducted into the Women Songwriters Hall of Fame.

Roberta in concert, 1971

Creative Management Associates and John Levy Enterprise

ACKNOWLEDGMENTS

Ever grateful to editor Anne Schwartz for her passion for this project and her sterling guidance. I would also be remiss if I did not thank editorial assistant Anne-Marie Varga, copy editor Alison Kolani, designer Sarah Hokanson, and everyone who helped bring this book to life.

Thank you to Suzanne Mino Koga, my personal manager and dear friend, for never giving up on my dream to share the story of my first piano with children.

Thank you to literary agent Jennifer Lyons for believing in this book from the start.

For filling in some blanks and sharing memories and stories about "little me," thank you to my niece Carol Hovey, my longtime friend James Whitmore, and especially my youngest sister Ingrid Flack Hunter, who, sadly, did not live to see this book's publication.

Thank you to Tonya Bolden for giving my story life, for giving "little me" a bright and beautiful voice, and for caring so much about the truth and authenticity of everything this story is about.

Thank you to Hayden Goodman for your beautiful illustrations that bring to life the story of "little me," capturing my curiosity, joy, and exuberance to have my very own piano.

Thank you to my mother, for seeing my talent, believing in me, and finding opportunity and guidance for me when I needed it most. Thank you to my father for my first piano—for all that it took to get it, move it, paint it, tune it—the start of my true life in music.

I love you and am forever grateful to you all.

—R.F.